MILTON'S PARADISE

A Comedy in One Act

by

Philip Stagg

Published by:
New Playwrights' Network
35 Sandringham Road
Macclesfield
SK10 1QB
Cheshire

ISBN 0 86319 290 4

CHARACTERS

Milton Brownslow

Richard Addison

Kate Spicer

Owen Spicer

Thea Potter

Simon Potter

Barry

Millie

The home of the Spicers. Time: the present

This play was first performed by the Arena Theatre Company at Birmingham Old Repertory Theatre, 1990.

MILTON'S PARADISE

Front of tabs, MILTON BROWNSLOW enters carrying a can of lager. He is greeted by raucous cheering, wild applause. He stands C. grinning at the audience, drinking in the ovation and the lager.

After some seconds, he holds up a hand for silence. The cheering ends abruptly. He cups one hand to his left ear. Birdsong is heard. He cups a hand to his right ear. Harps play. MILTON's grin widens. Again he holds up a hand for instantaneous silence. He turns to face the tabs and slowly raises his arms. The curtain goes up simultaneously. As it does so, MILTON turns back to the audience, grinning smugly. He makes a clumsy bow, inviting us to enter his 'paradise'. As MILTON steps back, melting into the darkness of the room beyond, the light on him dissolves into the dancing beam of a cine projector.

The room is comfortable and cluttered, tasteful but not expensive. There is a door C. to the kitchen, another R. to the hallway and the rest of the house, and patio windows L. leading to a garden. This is little more than a small corner with a bench.

Everyone in the room is seen in flickering silhouette as they watch the film being projected onto a screen in a corner of the room. Seated in various attitudes of interest or boredom are KATE SPENCER, her husband OWEN, and their guests.

SIMON and THEA POTTER, like the SPICERS, are in their early forties. Operating the projector is RICHARD ADDISON, a bachelor in his mid-forties. Never far from RICHARD is BARRY,

a nervously energetic man in his late twenties. MILTON is KATE's elder brother. He is a raw, expatriate Englishman now domiciled in Australia who has cultivated the accent of his adopted country to an absurd extent. In the darkness, as MILTON gropes his way to a seat, there is a muffled cry of protest as he steps on SIMON's feet. The film they are watching is of a recent garden party to celebrate MILTON's arrival for his annual holiday in England. The Spicers, the Potters and assorted family and friends can be seen, but largely the film is of MILTON himself who, as in the play, is permanently attached to a can of lager. He has contrived to appear in almost every shot; lurching drunkenly into view, kissing reluctant women, and mugging at the camera. MILTON, watching keenly from the settee, greets his every appearance with a whoop of delight.
As the film proceeds, KATE, unseen by the others, gets up and moves into the garden, switching on an exterior light. In contrast to the forced jollity of her guests, KATE's mood is one of extreme sadness. She leans heavily on the wall of the house and is close to tears. But the emotion instantly evaporates as another rifle-burst of MILTON's laughter reaches her. She turns angrily from the house and sits on the bench. Inside, the film has come to an end)

RICHARD: Thank you, Barry. *(BARRY, who has moved to a wall switch, turns on the lights as everyone stands or stretches, muttering polite comments such as "well done, Richard", and "very nice". It is clear, however, that only MILTON has enjoyed himself)* Oh, a bit amateurish, I'm afraid. Not up to my usual standard. But then, these special occasions are just a matter of record. Difficult to be very creative.

MILTON: Well, I thought it was bonzer.

OWEN: You would. You were the only one in it.

MILTON: It was my party, wasn't it? What's the point in throwin' a welcome barbie for a bloke if yer don't get a good dekko at the star guest? Who wants to look at your miserable mug anyway? The day yer crack yer face yer ears'll fall off. *(OWEN is embarrassed, but merely grins as he does at all MILTON's insults)*

RICHARD: Milton has a point, actually. Every film should have a purpose. And as the purpose of *this* film was to celebrate Milton's arrival, it's only right that he should be the focal point.

MILTON: You said it, Dickie boy.

RICHARD: I prefer Richard, actually.

OWEN: Focal point? The only time we saw anyone else was when he put his can of lager down, which wasn't often.

MILTON: Yer gettin' a bit uppity, aren't yer?

OWEN: Me?

MILTON: No, the queen o' bloody Sheba. Give it a rest, will yer? All this whingin's turnin' me grog sour. Nice way to treat yer brother-in-law, I must say. The trouble with you is yer stone jealous. I come good like a movie star and you're up there poncin' around lookin' a real drongo. Face it, Owen - a borin' old history teacher like you's no threat to Robert Redford, is he? Yer've got about as much star quality as a piece o' boiled fish. *(SIMON, who has been holding his stomach in discomfort, moves to the hall door)*

SIMON: Excuse me.

THEA: Where are you off to?

SIMON: The bathroom.

THEA: I hope you're not going to be sick again.

MILTON: *(Laughing)* That's sheilas for yer, mate. Can't even sneak off for a chunder without askin' permission.

THEA: You don't have to live with his stomach. All the beer he's had he won't get a wink of sleep. And who'll have to sit up with him all night? It won't be you, will it?

MILTON: Bloody 'ope not.

THEA: It's slow poison to him, beer. Slow poison. I don't know why he does it. It'd be quicker if he slashed his wrists.

SIMON: I'm not going to be sick. I just want a pee.

THEA: That's what you *say*. That's what he always *says*.

MILTON: Off yer go, mate. Pee leave granted.

THEA: And while you're up there have a look at the shower curtain.

SIMON: Why?

THEA: Because if you like it I might get one the same. *(Exit SIMON)* It'd be quicker if he just slashed his wrists.

MILTON: 'Ere, Dickie boy - what about runnin' that film again? I'm sure we'd all like another Captain Cook at it. *(This suggestion is greeted by a general buzz of alarm from everyone except BARRY who is changing the plug on the projector)*

RICHARD: Well, I don't know....

THEA: Actually, I think Kate might want to serve supper now.

OWEN: That's right....where is Kate?

MILTON: Tucker! Now there's a beaut idea. I'm so 'ungry I could eat a dead dingo's dangler. Could I ever. *(Exit OWEN to the kitchen)*

THEA: I hope Simon's all right.

MILTON: No worries, love. Unless he's been slygroggin'. I bet the boy's had no more than a couple o' tinnys all night. Mind you, I never met a pom yet who could hold his beer....*(Enter OWEN)* Look at Owen, there. A one-pot screamer if ever I saw one. *(OWEN moves to the hall door)*

OWEN: She must be upstairs....unless she's in the garden. Did anyone see her go out?

MILTON: Wherever she is, tell 'er to rattle 'er dags. I'm bloody starvin'. *(OWEN crosses to the patio doors L.)* An' no dawdlin' in the rose beds, neither. Not much danger there, I suppose. From what my sis says a eunuch with lumbago's more of a Casanova than he is. Yer should get loaded more often, mate. Might put some shot in yer pistol. *(MILTON laughs. OWEN turns angrily. He seems to be on the point of challenging MILTON, but then loses his nerve and grins. He goes out into the garden. On seeing him, KATE moves further along the bench, her back to him)*

OWEN: What are you doing out here?

KATE: Isn't it obvious? As soon as I've tuned these

bagpipes I'm going to play The Bluebells of Scotland.

OWEN: Look, I'm not enjoying this anymore than you. We couldn't put them off so let's get it over with. They'll be gone in a couple of hours then you can do what you like.

KATE: I came out for some air, that's all. I'm not trying to avoid anyone - apart from you. *(THEA pours herself a drink)*

THEA: *(To MILTON)* I really don't think you should needle Owen so much. He's very sensitive, you know, and he's definitely not himself tonight.

MILTON: He looks the same dozy prawn to me. Don't be a wowser, love. He knows I'm just havin' some fun with 'im. He loves it. Besides, he needs shakin' up. He's like the rest of 'em over 'ere. No offence, o' course, but most poms couldn't find their arse with a searchlight.

RICHARD: I thought you were born in Manchester.

MILTON: That was centuries ago. Soon as I saw the life out in Oz I said to meself - Milt, this is for you. Honest mate, over there it's a man's life. *(MILTON, THEA and RICHARD leap in alarm at the sound of a resonant, girlish squeal, like chalk being drawn across a slate. After some seconds, they realise that BARRY is laughing)* He's electrocuted himself. I knew he would.

RICHARD: What's the matter, Barry?

BARRY: It was just him saying that it's a man's life. It struck me...it struck me as funny. *(BARRY emits another screech)*

MILTON: What's funny about that?

BARRY: It depends how you look at it, of course...but when you consider that Australia has more homosexuals than any other country in the Western hemisphere....*(He releases another jarring peal. MILTON, scandalized, glowers at BARRY. RICHARD looks distinctly uneasy)*

OWEN: Are you coming inside or not? They're waiting to eat.

KATE: It's all ready.They can help themselves, can't they? *(OWEN sits on the bench beside KATE, who retreats even further)*

OWEN: There won't be much to help themselves to once your pig of a brother has buried his snout in the trough. I never realised it before but Milton's completely in proportion - a permanently empty brain balanced by a permanently bulging stomach.

KATE: Well, you won't have to worry about feeding him anymore, will you? Not after tonight.

OWEN: No, thank God.

KATE: When are you going to tell him? Or aren't you? Perhaps that's a little job you're planning to leave to me.

OWEN: Of course I'm going to tell him.

KATE: When?

OWEN: Tonight.

KATE: Tonight?

OWEN: Tonight.

KATE: That I'd like to see.

OWEN: Just once why don't you say it out straight? You think I'm scared of that loud-mouthed, beer-swilling yob.

KATE: Why should I think that? I mean - he's been here almost a week and hasn't missed a single opportunity to insult and belittle you, like he's done every summer for the past eight years. But like every summer for the past eight years you put him firmly in his place, don't you? The way you stand up to him manfully, look him straight in the eye and grin. Frankly, I'm surprised he doesn't run screaming into the street, one glimpse of that terrifying smile of yours.

OWEN: He's your brother, isn't he? A guest in my house?

KATE: No, Owen - *you're* the guest. It ceased to be *your* house the day you walked up to the doormat and said, "Move over, pal, there's room for two." *(BARRY, having completed re-wiring the plug, throws it to RICHARD)*

BARRY: There - good as new.

RICHARD: It was good as new before. I really don't know why you had to change it.

BARRY: You didn't see the wiring. Lethal. I shouldn't be surprised if every plug in the house was the same. Lots of little timebombs ticking away. *(BARRY begins dismantling the projector)*

RICHARD: I'd hardly describe a 13 amp plug as a timebomb.

BARRY: That's probably what three thousand people in Britain say every year before they plug in the iron and light up like a Christmas tree. You're too trusting, Ritchie.

RICHARD: I'd rather you didn't call me that.

BARRY: You come into a strange house with all this high-voltage equipment without a thought for your safety. It's a good job I'm here to look after you.

RICHARD: I don't need anyone to look after me thank you.... and what on earth are you doing now?

BARRY: That's exactly what I'm doing - checking the earth on this projector. Like it or not, Ritchie, I mean to watch out for you. You're a precious commodity. *(RICHARD, squirming with embarrassment, turns to MILTON who is leering at them both)*

RICHARD: *(With forced laughter)* He's a scream, isn't he?

MILTON: He's a bloody riot - *(winking)* precious.

OWEN: I might not be perfect, but at least I don't go around discussing our sex life with everyone.

KATE: What sex life?

OWEN: There you are. Evidently that's what you've been telling Milton. From the vulgar remarks he's just been making, it seems like you've had a good long talk with him about it.

KATE: You fall for it every time, don't you? He throws you some bait and you swallow it down hook, line and sinker. I can assure you, Owen, that if I ever chose to discuss our so-called sex life with anyone, which I haven't, it wouldn't need a good long talk. It would all be over in a couple of minutes. *(MILTON places a hand on RICHARD's and BARRY's shoulders)*

MILTON: Yer know, it's about time you two got it together.

RICHARD: *(Alarmed)* I beg your pardon?

MILTON: This cine stuff. I know yer rapt an' I don't wanna rubbish it, but it's straight off the bloody Ark, mate. Video - that's the apples these days.

RICHARD: Video! The idiot's delight!

MILTON: Are you slingin' me off?

RICHARD: No, no...I'm not saying video cameras aren't a technological wonder. But without absurdly expensive editing, they're little more than glorified snapshot machines. Everything comes out all joined up in the order you shoot it.

BARRY: But with cine film.....

RICHARD: Thank you, Barry. As president of the cine club, I rather think it falls to me to explain the merits of the cinematic art.

BARRY: And no-one does it better than you, Ritchie.

MILTON: *(To RICHARD)* I think he likes yer.

RICHARD: What you must remember is that nature's a shapeless thing. It's the camera that gives it shape. Take nature's own opening scene - a sunrise.

MILTON: Beaut.

RICHARD: But not very shapely.

MILTON: I don't know how many times I've said the same thing.

RICHARD: But film that sunrise framed by an open window, or reflected in a puddle, better still across a field of sunflowers - symbolic see? - and the whole thing becomes a living portrait.

MILTON: But could yer make the sun rise over a tinny?

RICHARD: A what?

MILTON: Tin o' lager. Now that'd be worth seein'. *(In the garden, OWEN stands)*

OWEN: All right, I'll prove it to you. I'll prove once and for all I'm not scared of any artless Aussie ape. I'll go in there right now and tell him he has to leave. Tonight.

KATE: Of course you will, Owen.

OWEN: You don't believe me?

KATE: If you say so.

OWEN: I do say so.

KATE: Fine. That's settled then.

OWEN: Right. *(OWEN moves to the door and hesitates)*

RICHARD: There's no great mystery, of course. After all, a basic camera's just a film counter, transporter claw, gate, viewfinder, cartridge, diaphragm, lens, filming button, cable release....

BARRY: What about exposing everything?

RICHARD: What?

BARRY: The exposure meter...you forgot about that.

RICHARD: I don't think you need put it quite like that, Barry.

OWEN: Well, aren't you coming with me? *(KATE stands)*

KATE: I didn't realise you wanted me to hold your hand.

OWEN: Of course not. You're going to see this. You're going to remember it. That brother of yours has insulted me for the last time and I want everyone to know it.

KATE: Oh, for God's sake.... *(KATE pushes OWEN aside and enters the living room)* Supper everyone?

MILTON: 'Bout ruddy time. I thought I was gonna be stuck wi' Cecil B. de bloody Mille all night. *(There is a general movement towards the kitchen door as OWEN enters from the garden)*

OWEN: Just a minute. I have something to say. *(They all stare at him in silent expectation)*

MILTON: Well, what are yer waitin' for - a roll on the drums?

OWEN: No, I.....

MILTON: Strewth, what a dill. Spit it out, will yer? The grub's goin' cold an' yer standin' there lookin' like a hooked mackerel. *(Enter SIMON from the hall looking even more bilious than before, his clothes and hair dishevelled)*

THEA: I knew it. He's been sick.

SIMON: I couldn't help it, Thea. Honestly I couldn't.

THEA: Of course you can help it. If you didn't sit guzzling down poison all night there wouldn't be a problem, would there? *(SIMON suddenly begins clearing his nose and throat, an explosion of racks, spits and hacking sounds. Everyone except THEA retreats in alarm)* Don't panic. It's only his sinuses. If he doesn't do that he's as deaf as a post in the morning.

MILTON: What we're all dyin' to know is what he thought o' the shower curtain.

SIMON: That's the embarrassing thing, really.

THEA: *(With dread)* Why is it embarrassing?

SIMON: I was sick on it.

THEA: Oh God....

SIMON: Only a little bit, but I thought I'd better mention it. I really couldn't help it. The shower cubicle's right next to the lavatory, you see, and as I leaned over....

THEA: I don't think we need any details, Simon, thank you. It's very thoughtful of you, but I'm sure we'll all manage quite nicely without a graphic description. *(Turning up her sleeves)* Well - enjoy yourselves everyone. It seems I've got an appointment with a bottle of ammonia. Perhaps that's what people mean when they invite us to a bring-a-bottle party.

SIMON: It's all right. I've cleaned up.

THEA: From past experience, Simon, all you've done is wave a sponge in the air. *(THEA moves to the kitchen door)*

KATE: Go and have something to eat with the others, Thea. I'll see to it later.

THEA: Certainly not. I'm the one who married an active volcano, not you.

(Exit THEA to kitchen)

SIMON: I'm sorry about this, Kate. I didn't mean to spoil the party.

KATE: Don't be silly. You haven't spoiled anything.

OWEN: Apart from the shower curtain.

KATE: It's not Simon's fault if he suffers from a nervous stomach.

OWEN: He suffers from everything. In all the years we've known him I don't remember once when he wasn't at death's door with something or other. I'm surprised he hasn't got a personal entry in Black's Medical Dictionary.

SIMON: It's true. I don't enjoy the best of health.

OWEN: The *best* of health? *(To the others)* When he moved house three years ago the local chemist closed down. *(Enter THEA. She is wearing rubber gloves and carries a bucket, cloth and cleaning fluids)*

SIMON: Oh no....not the bucket, Thea. It's humiliating.

THEA: You should have thought of that before you poured gallons of toxic slop into your system.

KATE: I wish you'd leave it, Thea.

THEA: Stop worrying, Kate. I'm used to it. Simon and me have the ideal marriage. We both know our places - his is bent double over the toilet, mine's standing right behind him with a mop and bucket. It's been like that for fifteen years so why change the act now? The only thing that puzzles me is that after all that target practice you'd think his aim would be perfect. Don't think I'm complaining. In fact, if I went home after a party *without* having scrubbed the carpet, the sink or the shower tray I'd almost feel I'd missed something. Perhaps that's why I take such an interest in bathroom fittings. *(THEA turns to the hall door)*

KATE: Thea, if you insist on doing this, there's a bucket in the landing cupboard.

THEA: Fine. I'll leave this one with Simon. *(She places the bucket over SIMON's head)* And if that doesn't stop him drinking any more beer, it'll be nice and handy when he starts feeling queasy again. And Kate - one little favour. When you serve supper, watch him like a hawk, would you? If he goes near the prawns cut his hands off. *(Exit THEA to the hall. SIMON crosses to the settee and sits dejectedly. Without removing the bucket, he puts his head in hands)*

MILTON: Well, I don't know about anyone else, but all this gasbaggin's given me a rare old appetite. Bit o' cold chook, I think, followed by a nice big dollop o' my sis's beaut sherry trifle. *(SIMON groans)* Oh - I was forgettin'. Owen's gonna make a speech, aren't yer mate? *(OWEN glances at KATE who is watching him challengingly)*

OWEN: It's....not very important.

MILTON: Never thought it would be.The day a prize galah like you's got anythin' worth listenin' to I'll put out the bloody flags. *(Exit MILTON to the kitchen. BARRY closes up the projector and wipes his hands)*

BARRY: There. Filthy dirty, I'm afraid, but electrically sound. Something to eat, Ritchie?

RICHARD: Later maybe - and I've asked you not to call me that.

BARRY: Well, I shouldn't wait too long if I were you. I know - I'll prepare a little plate for you. Bit of salad, some cheese - and I bet you'd like a nice big sausage?

RICHARD: I'll get my own food, thank you.

BARRY: As you like. *(BARRY moves to the kitchen door)* I'm just trying to prove to you how indispensable I am, Ritchie. Believe me, the day will come when you'll wonder how you ever managed without me. *(Exit BARRY)*

KATE: Come on, Simon. It isn't that bad. *(KATE tries to remove the bucket from SIMON's head but he stops her)*

SIMON: I'd rather keep it on, thanks. I'm too embarrassed to face anyone.

KATE: Well, we can't talk to a bucket all night. Look - come into the kitchen and get something to eat.

SIMON: I daren't.

KATE: Of course you can. You might feel better if you try something light. *(SIMON allows KATE to lead him to the kitchen door. He pauses)*

SIMON: This bucket smells funny.

KATE: I'm not surprised. That's the one we normally keep horseshit in for the garden. *(KATE steers SIMON through the kitchen door)* By the way, Owen - impressive performance. The way you just waded in like that, there were a couple of times I was afraid I might actually swoon. *(Exit KATE to kitchen)*

RICHARD: Isn't she feeling well?

OWEN: She was being sarcastic, Richard.

RICHARD: Yes, well you know what they say about sarcasm.

OWEN: No.

RICHARD: No, neither do I now. But it's something really clever. *(RICHARD hovers by the kitchen door)*

OWEN: Why don't you go and get something to eat?

RICHARD: I wanted a word, actually.

OWEN: Not now, Richard. D'you mind?

RICHARD: It won't take long. It's about Barry.

OWEN: Nice boy.

RICHARD: Oh, hell!

OWEN: What?

RICHARD: You really think he's a nice boy?

OWEN: Isn't he?

RICHARD: I suppose so. I mean, he seems *nice* enough, but when you say "nice *boy*" like that, it rather implies that he's....well, a *nice boy.*

OWEN: A shirt-lifter, you mean?

RICHARD: I don't know and that's what bothers me. You see, he keeps following me around. I can't take a step without him breathing down my neck. It's like having an extra shadow.

OWEN: Worrying.

RICHARD: Terrifying. When he first joined the cine club it seemed like a God-send. I mean, he's an absolute genius with his screwdriver, a terrific electrician. The trouble is...

OWEN: Is he AC or DC?

RICHARD: Quite. I could be imagining things, of course. But it's the way he's latched on to me, like an assistant. At first, it was just phoning me all the time. Now he virtually waits on the doorstep. When I came out tonight there he was sitting in the car, fiddling with his soldering iron.

OWEN: Unpleasant.

RICHARD: Unnerving. I had to bring him with me. I couldn't think of an excuse not to.

OWEN: You could always tell him to sod off.

RICHARD: I could, yes...but there's the risk that it might hurt his feelings, and he looks up to me so. I feel haunted, Owen, haunted.

OWEN: I don't see what I can do.

RICHARD: What really worries me is that people will get the wrong impression. They might think that I welcome his attentions and I don't, Owen, really I don't. Just because I'm not married....well, people assume that when a chap's single...and I'm not. As you know, I used to live with a woman. It was only for a fortnight, but still.

OWEN: Richard, you don't have to defend your sexuality to me.

RICHARD: I'm not on trial, Owen. I'm just trying to make you understand how easily people get the wrong idea. You've known me for years, but what do strangers think when they see me being followed around by a nice boy who calls me Ritchie and offers me a sausage on a plate?

OWEN: Dangerous.

RICHARD: Horrendous.

OWEN: I still think you're worrying about nothing. Y ou're straight, Richard.

RICHARD: That's it. If anyone ever suggests anything about me behind my back I want you to put them *straight*. Will you do that?

OWEN: Of course. I'll get everyone together now if you like and make an announcement. Ladies and gentlemen, Mr Richard Addison would like it to be known that, contrary to appearances, he and Torchy the Battery Boy are just good friends. *(RICHARD turns away in anger)* All right, stop fretting.

RICHARD: A last favour. If you see Barry engage me in a corner...

OWEN: I'll have you both arrested.

RICHARD: In conversation. I'd be grateful if you could distract his attention, just long enough for me to escape.

OWEN: It's funny really.

RICHARD: I'm glad you think so.

OWEN: I mean - we're in a similar predicament. We're both dogged by someone who's making our lives a misery. And instead of confronting the problem, we back off all the time, run away. What d'you say, Richard?

Shall we stop running? Shall we turn and fight? *(Enter KATE from the kitchen)*

KATE: If you want something to eat you'd better make it quick. They're cleaning plates faster than a turbo-charged dishwasher in there. *(RICHARD turns towards the kitchen door) You* don't need to panic, Richard. Barry's standing guard over a plate of sausage rolls. He's quite a little treasure, isn't he? *(RICHARD glances at OWEN, who nods encouragingly)*

RICHARD: *(Determinedly)* You're right, Kate. That's exactly what he is. And it's high time someone buried him. *(RICHARD strides to the kitchen door, squares his shoulders and goes out)*

KATE: Well, I don't know what all that was about, but it's nice to see someone in this house is capable of positive action. *(Enter THEA from the hall)*

THEA: *(Peeling off her rubber gloves)* D'you know, Kate, I've lost count of the times I must have scrubbed that bathroom. If I didn't know you better I'd swear you only invited us round to get the place cleaned up.

OWEN: Excuse me. *(OWEN goes out into the garden)*

THEA: What did I say?

KATE: *(Distractedly, looking off into the garden)* Sorry?

THEA: Is my animal attraction wearing off or have you been having words?

KATE: Words?

THEA: Kate, what *is* the matter? The pair of you have been limping around like wounded bears all night.

KATE: Everything's fine. And don't worry about Simon. I put him in the corner with some fruit salad. He can't come to much harm with that.

THEA: Simon would come to grief on an egg custard. It's you I'm worried about. *(KATE sits on an arm of the settee)*

KATE: Do you still love him?

THEA: Simon? That's a bit below the belt, isn't it? For a question like that I need a week's notice at least.

KATE: I mean - is he the same man you married?

THEA: Good God, no. Mind you, we've always had a sort of

patient-nurse relationship. He likes to be nursed and I try to be patient. I know I tend to over-mother him. I suppose that's because we never had any kids. There was some difficulty, you see...with Simon's sperm count.

KATE: What difficulty?

THEA: You couldn't count on it.

KATE: Thea, I'm trying to be serious.

THEA: Then for heaven's sake stop dragging Simon into it. *(KATE stands, crosses to a drinks table and pours a glass of wine)* But we're not really talking about *my* marriage, are we?

KATE: You stay with him. You obviously still care for him.

THEA: Oh..he has his moments. Sometimes when we're in bed, I turn on the light and lie there looking at him. And occasionally, very occasionally, when he doesn't smell of Vick and the bedside table isn't littered with tissues and bottles of Night Nurse, I can almost see him like he was. And I think...well...he'll do.

KATE: That's *it?* My God, Thea, is that *all?* We try to remember how it *was*? I'm forty-three years old. Forty bloody three! And you're telling me the best is over? *(OWEN, who has been sitting on the garden bench, gets up and steps towards the house. The intensity of the women's voices causes him to hesitate. He stands listening in the doorway, unseen)*

THEA: Of course not. But you have to accept that people change.

KATE: Like Simon.

THEA: No, some people change for the better. Look - why don't you just tell me what Owen's done?

KATE: I wish there was something to tell. He sees the problem and pulls his head in like a turtle. But the worst of it is I don't know if he's afraid or just doesn't care. Thea, we live like brother and sister. And we don't even commit incest anymore.

THEA: This problem - it's got a name?

KATE: It's got a name. *(MILTON stumbles on from the*

kitchen. He is now slightly the worse for drink. Between pulling on a can of lager he gnaws a chicken leg. His shirt-front bears evidence of earlier courses)

MILTON: That's what I call a pig-out. You've done me proud, sis. Bloody proud. *(KATE hurries past him into the kitchen)* Where's she goin'? This is supposed to be a party - Rafferty's Rules. I come out here 'cause I'm jacked off wi' lookin' at that sickbag of a husband o' yours and' a couple o' poofters havin' a lovers' tiff an' it's no bloody better. Why's everyone gone snaky all of a sudden? *(THEA tries to pass him. He blocks the kitchen doorway)* Not you too, love. Why don't yer stay here wi' me an' have some fun?

THEA: What did you have in mind?

MILTON: Yer a real looker, Thea. I've always thought so. You an' me, we deserve a good time. So what I'm thinkin' is that if you ever fancy a real man some arvo when that chunder-box yer married is off to work, well...I'm only a couple o' streets within cooee o' your place.

THEA: That's a very interesting suggestion. I'll have to give it some thought.

MILTON: You do that. Only don't take too long about it, eh? *(THEA exits to the kitchen. MILTON, having finished the chicken leg, looks around the room for somewhere to dispose of it. Finding nowhere, he lifts a seat on the settee and throws it under there. Still hungry, MILTON scoops up a handful of peanuts from a bowl on the coffee table as OWEN steps into the room)*

OWEN: Drop them.

MILTON: *(Startled)* Yer dozy nong! What d'yer wanna go sneakin' up like that for?

OWEN: I said put those nuts down. You've had your last meal at my expense.

MILTON: Are you off yer scone?

OWEN: No, you are. Scones, sherry trifle...*(he retrieves the chicken bone from under the settee and drops it at MILTON's feet)*.....chicken legs....*(he knocks the peanuts from MILTON's hand)*....peanuts...*(he snatches MILTON's can of lager)*...and beer. The only thing you'll get from me is a cup of coffee before you go in the morning.

MILTON: Go where?

OWEN: As long as it's a thousand miles from me I couldn't care less. The holiday, Milton, is over. This year, next year, every year. You'll be delighted to hear that your sister and the no-hoper she married are splitting up.

MILTON: Since when?

OWEN: Since about eight years ago, which by a not altogether bizarre coincidence is exactly when you started honouring us with your delightful annual visits.

MILTON: 'Ave you been playin' up? 'Cause if you've been cheatin' on my lovely sis I'll knock yer ruddy block off.

OWEN: Of course, to a man like you that could be the only possible explanation.

MILTON: What's that mean - a man like me?

OWEN: An uncultured, insensitive yob who's incapable of feeling anything that doesn't connect with his mouth or his John Thomas.

MILTON: You'd better talk to me proper.

OWEN: For the first time in all the miserable years I've known you that's exactly what I'm trying to do - talk to you proper-ly.

MILTON: Then keep my John Thomas out of it.

OWEN: Milton, don't take this personally, but you are without doubt the most uncouth, the most unprepossessing blob of dubious humanity that ever drew breath between slurps of Castlemaine bloody Four X.

MILTON: *(Snatching back his lager can)* It's Fosters.

OWEN: You're a caricature. A belching, bumptious, blustering burlesque of a man whose grasp on reality amounts to putting a vice-like grip on a knife and fork. You're the worst character from an Australian soap opera come hideously to life, and you're ridiculous accent's so thick you could throw a very large boomerang round it. If ever one man embodied every argument for dissolving the Commonwealth it's you.

MILTON: Finished?

OWEN: Only 'till I get my breath back.

MILTON: Well make it quick 'cause the minute yer done I'm gonna rip your nose off.

OWEN: Then you'd better do it now. I've got eight years of insults to throw back at you and I'm only just finding my aim.

MILTON: Right now?

OWEN: Right now.

MILTON: Hold this. *(MILTON hands his lager to OWEN and begins rolling up his sleeves. As he does so, OWEN drinks from the can. Horrified, MILTON seizes the can and shakes it)* You've drained the bugger.

OWEN: I paid for it.

MILTON: Yeah, but yer don't go 'an...that's right. Strewth, I never thought o' that. I can't hit someone who's bought me grog.

OWEN: Oh, don't let that stop you. It's a bit late for a sudden attack of principles, isn't it?

MILTON: I've got principles, all right. Principles you poms wouldn't understand. An' one of 'em is yer don't clobber a bloke who's paid for yer beer.

OWEN: Why not? I pay for everything else. I pay for the mountains of food you empty into your gullet with all the finesse of an earth shovel.

MILTON: I'm fond o' me tuck. I don't say I'm not.

OWEN: Fond? That's like saying a sperm whale's vaguely partial to plankton. Why you've never exploded is one of the mysteries of medical science. Whenever you get up from the table I'm always afraid you'll bump into something sharp and pebbledash the walls. That isn't the half of it. I pay for the cigars permanently sticking out of your face. I even pay for the petrol you use driving *my* car to the pub every day so you can come back even more revolting than when you left. So please - don't let's be dainty over one can of lager.

MILTON: Mean bugger, aren't yer? No wonder a beaut girl like my sis is dumpin' yer. Stands to reason now I think about it.

OWEN: You haven't understood a word, have you? The fact that you're beaut sis and me are on the brink of divorce is down to one person - you.

MILTON: Don't go puttin' any blame on my neck. If you're marriage has gone down the thunderbox that's your look-out. Just 'cause I like a few beers an' a bit o' funnin' around.....

OWEN: Is that what you call it? Tell me, Milton, on all these visits what's been your chief amusement - apart from pursuing a relentless ambition to wear larger trousers? I'll tell you, shall I? Humiliation. Mine. My job, my appearance, my lack of drinking prowess, my alleged sexual failings - it's all fair game, isn't it?

MILTON: Come off it, sport. I was just givin' yer the heaps.

OWEN: Well, whatever that means it wasn't a heap of fun.

MILTON: But yer never said nothin'.Whenever I looked at yer, yer gob was split like a paddy melon. If it got to yer, all that stuff, why didn't yer do somethin' about it?

OWEN: Why should I? Why should I put on some pathetic hero act? Can you imagine how degrading it is when you're expected to prove something you thought you'd proved years ago? I don't know...maybe Kate's right. Maybe I'm just spineless. The only reason I'm saying all this now is because it doesn't matter anymore.

MILTON: And I'm really the cause of it - all of it?

OWEN: Waiting for you to arrive every year is like living on Death Row. Except there you have a chance of getting the sentence commuted. The strange thing is, Kate never blames you. I suppose she accepts you for what you are. *(MILTON cracks open another can of lager and takes a couple of thoughtful swigs. For the first time he seems genuinely troubled)*

MILTON: I feel lousy.

OWEN: You are.

MILTON: I mean it, mate. I never realised I was comin'

between yer. I reckon that's a sort o' sin. What God joins together let no man put asunder.

OWEN: Why Milton, I had no idea the spirit moved within you. Except my whisky, of course.

MILTON: And all these years I've been.....asunderin'.

OWEN: If they ever write a song called Asundering Matilda they'll dedicate it to you.

MILTON: 'Course....*(he laughs)*...there is a funny side.

OWEN: I'm relieved.

MILTON: It's what yer call - ironical. I mean, if what you say's right, I come over 'ere an' make your life a misery. Yer can't call the place yer own and the wife thinks yer a sissy little ratbag. You have to laugh.....

OWEN: Perhaps I missed something.

MILTON: What I'm sayin' is...fifty weeks out of every year I'm in the same sorta boat as you, only mine's a lot rockier. The only peace I get is when I'm over 'ere. That's what I mean - ironical. We sorta swop places.

OWEN: I've definitely missed something. *(During the following speeches, MILTON drops his Australian accent)*

MILTON: You've never met my Joanie, have you?

OWEN: Joanie?

MILTON: The wife. You wouldn't forget something like that. Well, I'm not saying I don't think the world of her. But what I will say about Joanie is...she's difficult. And the trouble with living with a difficult woman is that life tends to get very.....

OWEN: Difficult?

MILTON: Bloody impossible. You know what I mean?

OWEN: What's happened to your voice?

MILTON: What voice?

OWEN: That voice. You're speaking English.

MILTON: Oh, the accent. I didn't realise I'd dropped it.

OWEN: I heard it land with a thud.

MILTON: *(Immediately recovering his accent)* Bit of a confession there, sport. I only talk Oz when I'm over 'ere. I daren't try the lingo back 'ome, they'd spot me for a dud straight off.

OWEN: You damned phoney!

MILTON: That's what I'm tryin' to tell yer. The accent's not the only thing that's phoney. Back 'ome I'm a teetotal, non-smokin' vegetarian.

OWEN: You expect me to believe that?

MILTON: Oh yes - my Joanie sees to that. It's like I was sayin'. Joanie's got very strong views on life. Difficult views. She explained it all to me just after we got wed. What she wanted, she said, was a particular type of 'usband, with particular attributes. Trouble was that after takin' a good dekko at me, the only attribute she could spot was that I changed my underpants every day. Still, I was a challenge, she said. Well, I'll say this - there 'asn't been a day gone by when Joanie 'asn't stuck to that challenge like shit to a sheep's arse. Now I'm not gonna deny Joanie her life's work, but it's no use. I'm a slob an' I like bein'a slob. It's what I was meant to be an' I feel comfortable with it. Back 'ome she 'as me jumpin' through ruddy hoops - I'm polite, considerate, well-mannered. Yer wouldn't know me. But inside I'm still a slob. That's why I gotta escape 'ere every year. I can swear, smoke, eat an' drink like a pig, be bloody rude - anythin' I want, an' there's no one to say "Stop it, Milton - that's not nice." Yer see what I'm gettin' at? This place o' yours, it's a garden o' bloody Eden.

OWEN: A garden of Eden? A garden of BLOODY EDEN? *(BARRY bursts on from the kitchen in a fury followed immediately by RICHARD)*

RICHARD: Barry, please don't be hasty. It was all a misunderstanding.

BARRY: I've never been so grossly insulted.

RICHARD: Listen to me. If you'd just let me explain.

BARRY: Don't speak to me. Don't speak to me ever again. *(Exit BARRY to the hall. RICHARD rushes after him)*

RICHARD: *(As he exits)* Barry, please. When I said I'm keeping my back to the wall I didn't mean...

OWEN: You sit there - you sit there and have the gall to tell me that because you're a congenital coward, too feeble to stand up to your grotesque wife, you come here and make *my* life unbearable?

MILTON: Fair go. I never meant it like that.

OWEN: You actually sit there and tell me that I've endured eight years of hell, eight years of humiliation that have brought my sanity and my marriage to the edge of ruin all because you like to play Macho Man for two weeks every summer?

MILTON: Well...

OWEN: You dare to sit there, on your fat backside, in my house, in my chair, in my favourite chair, and tell me without so much as a blush mantling your cheek, that I'm running some kind of Butlin's for emotionally battered husbands?

MILTON: Well, now yer mention it....

OWEN: *(Quietly)* I'm going to kill you. *(SIMON hurries on from the kitchen, both hands clamped over his mouth. He exits to the hall. Enter THEA from the kitchen followed by KATE)*

THEA: *(Calling after SIMON)* I'm warning you, my lad. Go near that shower curtain again and I won't be responsible.

KATE: You can't blame him this time, Thea. You shouldn't have said all those things.

THEA: It's my marriage, Kate. I'll handle it as I see fit. *(Exit THEA to the kitchen. KATE follows)*

KATE: *(As she exits)* I'm not suggesting you tell lies, but surely a tactful silence....*(MILTON, alarmed by the advancing OWEN, gets up and stands behind the armchair)*

MILTON: There's no point in gettin' snaky, mate. Now it's all out in the open, why don't we just sit down nice an' quiet an' have a few beers?

OWEN: I can't decide if you're evil or just a moron. *(They circle the armchair, OWEN in slow, steady pursuit)*
There's a sort of hideously clever cunning about what you've done. Almost premeditated malice. But then I look at that blank stupid face, and I hear

the wind whistling through that vacant skull....

MILTON: Don't come the raw prawn, Owen. Yer know I never meant any o' those things I said. Yer a bonzer bloke. One o' the best. *(OWEN makes a sudden move towards MILTON who retreats to the opposite end of the room)*

OWEN: Well, well....now we really have swapped places. *(Enter RICHARD from the hall. He is breathless)*

RICHARD: Has anyone seen Barry? He vanished round the side of the house and I can't find him anywhere. I mustn't let him go without an explanation. What if this gets out? What am I going to tell everyone at the cine club? *(Enter BARRY from the garden)* There you are, Barry. Thank goodness I found you. *(Ignoring RICHARD, BARRY begins collecting his screwdrivers and other tools from various parts of the room. RICHARD trails after him)* All right, I admit I've got a nasty, suspicious mind and you've every right to be cross. I apologise, humbly. I see now that your offer of friendship was pure and sincere. You mustn't think of leaving the cine club, you know. Your absence might be rather awkward to explain. *(BARRY shakes MILTON's hand)*

BARRY: Nice to have met you, Mr Brownslow.

RICHARD: You weren't thinking of leaving, were you? *(BARRY shakes OWEN's hand)*

BARRY: Thank you for your hospitality, Mr Spicer. *(BARRY moves to the hall door)*

RICHARD: If you go, who's going to be my chief projectionist? *(BARRY stops, half turns, encouraged)* Didn't I mention that? Oh yes, chief projectionist. And that's only to start with. Why don't we discuss it over dinner some night?

BARRY: When?

RICHARD: Oh, next month, perhaps? *(BARRY turns back to the hall door, quickly)* Tomorrow?

BARRY: Where?

RICHARD: My place?

BARRY: *(Smiling)* I'll wait for you in the car, Ritchie. *(Exit BARRY to the hall)*

RICHARD: I'll pick up my stuff tomorrow if that's all right, Owen. *(RICHARD moves to hall door. He turns, his relief giving way to doubt)* You don't suppose...I mean, you don't think that he's...? No, of course not. He's such a nice boy. *(Exit RICHARD to the hall. OWEN resumes his advance on MILTON. During the following exchanges, they negotiate the dining table, MILTON striving to keep it firmly between them)*

OWEN: You'll probably laugh, but I used to be intimidated by you. *(MILTON forces a laugh)* I said you'd find it amusing.

MILTON: But I wouldn't hurt a fly.

OWEN: That's where we differ. I've just discovered I have this latent streak of aggression and it's alarmingly powerful.

MILTON: You can get tablets for that.

OWEN: But I don't want tablets for it. I want to give it full rein, I want it to burst in a terrifying explosion of violence.

MILTON: I shouldn't do that.

OWEN: Why not? Don't you think I'll feel better afterwards? *(MILTON is now closest to the door R, OWEN on the opposite side of the table)*

MILTON: You'll feel terrible. I know you, Owen - you'll regret it.

OWEN: Perhaps you're right. Let's see, shall we? *(OWEN leaps onto the table-top in a desperate lunge at MILTON, who bolts for the door R)* Stop! *(MILTON halts at the door, unsure which way to go)* You're trapped, Milton Brownslow. Cornered in a hole like a frightened rabbit. There's nowhere to run. Whichever way you go they'll see you for what you are. Why don't you shout for help? Come on, Milton, don't be shy...good and loud...HELP, HELP, HELP! *(Enter KATE hurriedly from the kitchen)*

KATE: What the hell's going on....? *(seeing OWEN)* Oh, I see. Milton dear, if you *must* terrorise Owen I wish you'd do it some place where the furniture won't suffer. Or am I misjudging the situation? Perhaps

Owen saw a big bad mouse and you're trying to catch it for him. No, that can't be it. The only mouse in here is *on* the table. *(Exit KATE to the kitchen)*

MILTON: I said you'd regret it.

OWEN: If I threw myself off, d'you think I'd break anything vital?

MILTON: I'd like to help yer, sport, an' that's dinkum. I mean, I *could* tell Kate the whole bit - how yer rumbled me an' went for me like a maniac.

OWEN: You'd do that?

MILTON: No bloody chance. Think what it'd do to me reputation with the women. *(Enter KATE and THEA from the kitchen)*

KATE: Are you sure you have to go, Thea? It seems so early. We could watch some more films if you like....*(as she notices that OWEN is still on the table)*...unless Owen wants to show you the triple somersault with half-pike twist he's been practising? *(Enter SIMON from the hall)*

THEA: Well, Simon - feeling better now?

SIMON: I haven't been sick.

THEA: That *is* good news.

SIMON: I was just upset for a while. But I've been giving it a lot of thought and I know my duty.

THEA: I'm sure you do, Simon. I never doubted it for a second. *(SIMON crosses to MILTON)*

SIMON: *(Taking the can of lager from MILTON's hand)* Excuse me. *(SIMON slowly pours the lager over MILTON's head then gives him back the can)* And the next time you make an improper suggestion to my wife I'll stuff the can down your throat - sport. *(SIMON moves to the hall door)* I think we're ready to leave now, Thea. I'll back the car out, shall I?

THEA: You do that, sweetheart. I'll be right out. *(SIMON exits to the hall)* You see, Kate, I tell Simon everything. Well, let's say everything I *want* to tell him. I wouldn't try to give advice to anyone, but I do find that for a really stable marriage a bit of honesty works wonders. Simon may not be every woman's dream but, like I said, he has his moments.

(Exit THEA to the hall)

KATE: *(Following THEA off)* You're making a puddle, Milton. *(Exit KATE to the hall)*

OWEN: *(Clambering down from the table)* There's a moral here somewhere.

MILTON: Yeah? *(He shakes his lager can and sighs)*

OWEN: Well, think about Simon.

MILTON: I am.

OWEN: As his own wife says, not the answer to a maiden's prayer. In fact, I've heard more than one woman remark that she wouldn't have an affair with him if it meant averting World War Three. Still, I endure eight years of insults. He sorts you out in ten minutes. Impressive. *(Enter KATE from the hall. She throws a towel at MILTON)*

KATE: Upstairs with you. Into the shower.

MILTON: I don't think I'll bother with another one, love.

KATE: You're not staying here, messing up my living room.

MILTON: That's right. I'm not stayin' here, an' I won't be messin' up yer livin' room or anythin' else. Not any more. But yer know, it was ruddy great while it lasted. *(Exit MILTON to the hall)*

KATE: What does that mean?

OWEN: I imagine it means he's going upstairs to pack.

KATE: Pack? Surely he's not leaving because of that stupid incident with Simon?

OWEN: Oh no. Simon cooled him down. I turned on the tap. I've been having a little chat with that brother of yours. You could say I pointed out the error of his ways.

KATE: I don't believe you.

OWEN: No. I didn't think you would. *(MILLIE, MILTON's nineteen-year old daughter, enters from the garden. She is dressed in jeans and sweater, with a rucksack slung on her back)*

MILLIE: G'day, Auntie Kate. G'day, Uncle Owen.

KATE: Good....

OWEN: .....God.

MILLIE: Surprised to see me?

KATE: Millicent?

MILLIE: Is it ever.

OWEN: *Little* Millicent?

MILLIE: Yer favourite niece in livin' colour. Most people call me sand-groper nowadays, but you can call me Millie. Got any grog? I'm as dry as a kangaroo's crutch.....

KATE: But how did you get here?

MILLIE: Through the garden. Yer doorbell's crook.

KATE: I mean here, at the house.

MILLIE: Bushwalked. Yer know - hitched.

OWEN: From Canberra?

MILLIE: Heathrow, yer dill. *(To KATE)* Dad said he was a prawn. Where is Dad, by the way? Sleepin' off a gut-full, I'll bet. Don't worry, I know all about what he gets up to.

KATE: Is that so?

OWEN: Why do they call you sand-groper?

KATE: Millicent, I want to know exactly what you're doing here and I want to know now.

MILLIE: No worries, Auntie Kate. I'm not in any strife. I've got four weeks, see, before I start uni and I was really rapt to see England. Mum said it was a good idea so I could keep an eye on Dad. Some 'opes.

KATE: When you say keep an eye on him....

OWEN: You did say *four* weeks?

KATE: D'you mean keep an eye on him *here?*

OWEN: For *four* weeks?

MILLIE: Stop frettin', will yer? I won't be any trouble. Promise. I'm just like Dad - yer'll hardly know I'm around. *(KATE and OWEN exchange a glance of despair as MILTON enters from the hall carrying a travel bag. MILLIE is behind KATE and OWEN and at first he fails to notice her)*

MILTON: This is all I need for now, Kate. I'll arrange for the rest.....

MILLIE: Dad! *(MILLIE runs to MILTON and hugs him)*

MILTON: Millie! What the jumpin'jackeroo are you doin' here?

MILLIE: On me hols, same as you. I paid me own fare an' I don't start uni for four weeks.

OWEN: *(To KATE)* Does she have to keep saying that?

MILTON: Beauty. Just keep two spits an' a jump behind yer Dad an' we'll show these woolgrowers a thing or two. How's yer Mum, by the way?

MILLIE: Miserable bugger, same as always.

MILTON: That's my Joanie. *(OWEN has moved to the hall door)*

KATE: *(To OWEN)* What are you doing?

OWEN: Oh, nothing very much. It's just that I've been thinking for some time that I'd like to take a peek at Australia, and quite by chance I happen to know of a spare room that's vacant.

MILLIE: *(Spotting MILTON's travel bag)* Why the swag? Goin' somewhere?

MILTON: Now where would I be goin'? Course not - that's me dirty washin', love. Yer Auntie Kate's a very houseproud woman, Millie, an' insists on doin' me washin' every Saturday night regular.

MILLIE: *(Taking off her rucksack)* Beaut. She can do mine while she's at it.

KATE: Owen, that room....

MILLIE: *After* she gets me some tuck, I mean. 'Onest, Dad, I'm so 'ungry I could eat the bugs off a brumby's backside.

KATE: It wouldn't be a double, would it? *(OWEN smiles and stretches out a hand towards KATE. MILTON moves to the drinks table and picks up two cans of lager)*

MILTON: No worries there. This is sundowner city. Whatever yer want, just reach out and there it is.

MILLIE: *(Looking doubtfully around the room)* I dunno. Looks a bit of a dump to me. Are yer sure it's okay?

MILTON: Okay? *(MILTON gives MILLIE one of the cans. They remove the ring pulls)* It's paradise, love. Bloody paradise. *(KATE takes OWEN's hand. He pulls her to him in an embrace as MILTON and MILLIE raise their cans and drink deeply)*

THE END